10 MINUTE MOMENTS

parables

EXPLORING JESUS' PARABLES
10 MINUTES AT A TIME

D1053905

SCOTT
FIRESTONE IV

 simply for students

10-Minute Moments: Parables
Exploring Jesus' Parables 10 Minutes At a Time

Copyright © 2010 Scott Firestone IV
Visit our website: simplyyouthministry.com

Credits
Authors: Scott Firestone IV
Executive Developer: Nadim Najm
Chief Creative Officer: Joani Schultz
Editors: Rob Cunningham, Rick Lawrence
Cover Art Director: Riley Hall
Designer: Riley Hall
Production Manager: DeAnne Lear

Unless otherwise indicated, all Scripture quotations are taken from the Holy Bible,
New Living Translation, copyright © 1996, 2004, 2007. Used by permission of
Tyndale House Publishers, Inc., Carol Stream, Illinois 60188. All rights reserved.

978-0-7644-6351-8

10 9 8 7 6 5 4 3 2 1   17 16 15 14 13 12 11 10

Printed in the United States of America.

INTRODUCTION

I know it's a weird thing, but I don't really like when people call the accounts of the Bible *stories*. "Today we're going to talk about the story of Noah!" To me that makes them seem less real, like they didn't really happen—and believe me, they happened. But this might sound weird to you: I'm completely OK calling Jesus' parables *stories* because that's what these particular passages of Scripture contain.

The things in these stories didn't actually happen. Jesus telling these stories did happen.

So why did he use stories to get his points across? Well, think about some of your best memories—they're all connected to a story, right? Stories have the power to create vivid pictures—they help us remember important memories or truths. For instance, I have a hilarious story that helps me remember to always check whether I'm going into the men's or women's bathroom in a restaurant.

Jesus knew the power of stories, so he told stories that people of his time could relate to—stories about fishermen and seeds and sheep. But just because they were told to those first-century crowds doesn't mean there's nothing here for us to learn.

Sometimes the stories will be difficult to understand. Don't worry: Jesus had to explain them to his disciples, too. This book will help you understand Jesus' stories—what they meant to his audience and what they mean to your life—every day.

Now, who wants to hear a story?

Praying for you,

Scott Firestone IV

It's fitting that this is Jesus' first recorded parable; it's *foundational* to everything else he would say in his time on earth. It's easy to hear wise words, but the real wisdom comes in *applying* those words.

2 MINUTES

Read the passage below. Circle or underline any words/phrases/verses that you feel are important to remember.

Luke 6:46-49

⁴⁶"So why do you keep calling me 'Lord, Lord!' when you don't do what I say? ⁴⁷I will show you what it's like when someone comes to me, listens to my teaching, and then follows it. ⁴⁸It is like a person building a house who digs deep and lays the foundation on solid rock. When the floodwaters rise and break against that house, it stands firm because it is well built. ⁴⁹But anyone who hears and doesn't obey is like a person who builds a house without a foundation. When the floods sweep down against that house, it will collapse into a heap of ruins."

5 MINUTES

Think about the following questions and how they might apply to your life.

- You're not literally building a house, so what is Jesus talking about here?

1

- Think about one specific "floodwater" that has broken against your life. Was your response more like "standing firm" or more like "crumbling"? Explain. Why did you react the way you did?
- What does it mean to "dig deep and lay a foundation on solid rock"?
- Why isn't it enough to just hear Jesus' words? Doesn't that make us smart enough to avoid "floodwaters"?

Hanging out with God
- A house's foundation is what keeps it strong and solid. Having God as our foundation is the only way we can withstand life's floodwaters—and God wants nothing more than to be your foundation.
- Notice that Jesus doesn't say having a strong foundation means the floodwaters won't come.
- Ask God to help you not just listen to wise words, but to follow them as well.

Find a rock you can fit in your hand. Squeeze it; try to change its shape. Think about how your life might change if you were to build it on something solid, like the rock. Also, if you get the chance, take a walk on a gravel path—or gravel on a playground—and notice how difficult it is to keep your footing and maintain a solid base.

THOUGHTS

This space is here for you to jot down some thoughts, write out a prayer, draw a picture, or do whatever you want to help you remember your 10-minute moment.

Day 2

LOST SHEEP

Jesus was a controversial guy. He especially upset the Pharisees—a group of religious scholars who knew so much about religion that they completely missed the Savior of the universe in their midst. Making sure people followed the rules was very important to them—and Jesus' habit of hanging out with sinners definitely went against their rules. But their rules lacked love.

2 MINUTES

Read the passage below. Circle or underline any words/phrases/verses that you feel are important to remember.

Luke 15:1-10
¹Tax collectors and other notorious sinners often came to listen to Jesus teach. ²This made the Pharisees and teachers of religious law complain that he was associating with such sinful people—even eating with them!

³So Jesus told them this story: ⁴"If a man has a hundred sheep and one of them gets lost, what will he do? Won't he leave the ninety-nine others in the wilderness and go to search for the one that is lost until he finds it? ⁵And when he has found it, he will joyfully carry it home on his shoulders. ⁶When he arrives, he will call together his friends and neighbors, saying, 'Rejoice with me because I have found my lost sheep.' ⁷In the same way, there is more joy in heaven over one lost sinner who repents and returns to God than over ninety-nine others who are righteous and haven't strayed away!

[8]"Or suppose a woman has ten silver coins and loses one. Won't she light a lamp and sweep the entire house and search carefully until she finds it? [9]And when she finds it, she will call in her friends and neighbors and say, 'Rejoice with me because I have found my lost coin.' [10]In the same way, there is joy in the presence of God's angels when even one sinner repents."

Think about the following questions and how they might apply to your life.

- In what ways, if any, has Jesus pursued you in your life?
- How did you know it was Jesus pursuing you?
- Why do you think Jesus compares us to sheep?
- What might be the consequences of Jesus leaving the 99 to search for the one?
- Why is there so much joy over finding one lost sheep?

Hanging out with God
- If you are still a "lost sheep," consider coming to the One who loves you enough to pursue you. If you take that step, talk to your youth pastor about your decision.
- If you've committed your life to Jesus, ask God to bring to mind friends who haven't made the decision to follow Jesus—in other words, right now they're "lost." Imagine the party in heaven (and here on earth) when they are "found."
- How can you show your appreciation to Jesus for caring so much about you?

THOUGHTS

This space is here for you to jot down some thoughts, write out a prayer, draw a picture, or do whatever you want to help you remember your 10-minute moment.

Day 3

SHEEP AND THE GOATS

This is Jesus' last recorded parable. On one level it's Jesus telling us that one day there will be a judgment that we all must face. But beyond that, it's Jesus telling us that the way we live our lives ought to show love to others.

2 MINUTES

Read the passage below. Circle or underline any words/phrases/ verses that you feel are important to remember.

Matthew 25:31-46

³¹"But when the Son of Man comes in his glory, and all the angels with him, then he will sit upon his glorious throne. ³²All the nations will be gathered in his presence, and he will separate the people as a shepherd separates the sheep from the goats. ³³He will place the sheep at his right hand and the goats at his left.

³⁴"Then the King will say to those on his right, 'Come, you who are blessed by my Father, inherit the Kingdom prepared for you from the creation of the world. ³⁵For I was hungry, and you fed me. I was thirsty, and you gave me a drink. I was a stranger, and you invited me into your home. ³⁶I was naked, and you gave me clothing. I was sick, and you cared for me. I was in prison, and you visited me.'

³⁷"Then these righteous ones will reply, 'Lord, when did we ever see you hungry and feed you? Or thirsty and give you something to drink? ³⁸Or a stranger and show you hospitality? Or naked and give you clothing? ³⁹When did we ever see you sick or in prison and visit you?'

40"And the King will say, 'I tell you the truth, when you did it to one of the least of these my brothers and sisters, you were doing it to me!'

41"Then the King will turn to those on the left and say, 'Away with you, you cursed ones, into the eternal fire prepared for the devil and his demons. 42For I was hungry, and you didn't feed me. I was thirsty, and you didn't give me a drink. 43I was a stranger, and you didn't invite me into your home. I was naked, and you didn't give me clothing. I was sick and in prison, and you didn't visit me.'

44"Then they will reply, 'Lord, when did we ever see you hungry or thirsty or a stranger or naked or sick or in prison, and not help you?'

45"And he will answer, 'I tell you the truth, when you refused to help the least of these my brothers and sisters, you were refusing to help me.'

46"And they will go away into eternal punishment, but the righteous will go into eternal life."

5 MINUTES

Think about the following questions and how they might apply to your life.

- According to these verses, how does Jesus define "righteousness"?
- Why do you think Jesus places such emphasis on helping others?
- Jesus doesn't seem to dwell on rules and regulations. How is this different from the way people in our culture often understand or interpret Christianity?
- Does that mean rules and commandments have no place?
- What are some things you can do to take care of the hungry or the thirsty or the stranger or the "naked"?

3 MINUTES

Hanging out with God
- Think about someone in need that you may have ignored in the past. Ask God to forgive you for ignoring that person, and consider making it right with the individual.
- Ask God to show you people who are in need of your help and then give you the strength to follow through in helping them.
- Put it into practice. What can you do for someone tomorrow? Commit to accomplishing this task.

THOUGHTS

This space is here for you to jot down some thoughts, write out a prayer, draw a picture, or do whatever you want to help you remember your 10-minute moment.

Day 4

THE GROWING SEED

Farming is hard work. Preparing the ground. Tilling. Planting the seeds. Watering. Day. Night. Day. Night. A cycle that eventually produces a crop. So it is with our "farming" for the kingdom of God. It's really hard work, and we may never see the fruits of our labors, but that doesn't mean we've labored in vain. Our reward is in heaven.

2 MINUTES

Read the passage below. Circle or underline any words/phrases/ verses that you feel are important to remember.

Mark 4:26-29

[26]Jesus also said, "The Kingdom of God is like a farmer who scatters seed on the ground. [27]Night and day, while he's asleep or awake, the seed sprouts and grows, but he does not understand how it happens. [28]The earth produces the crops on its own. First a leaf blade pushes through, then the heads of wheat are formed, and finally the grain ripens. [29]And as soon as the grain is ready, the farmer comes and harvests it with a sickle, for the harvest time has come."

5 MINUTES

Think about the following questions and how they might apply to your life.

- What does this comparison tell you about the kingdom of God?
- Jesus says that the farmer doesn't understand what causes the seed to grow. What are some things you don't understand about faith and God?
- Are you OK with not understanding how the kingdom of God works but still believing it? Why or why not?

3 MINUTES

Hanging out with God

- Talk to God about your questions and about the things you don't understand. Ask God to put people and resources into your life that can get you closer to answers. But understand that not everything has an easy answer.
- Even though we might not know the exact reason a seed grows as it does, we can still see the results in a giant, strong redwood tree.

EXPERIENCE

Find a picture of a great big tree—or better yet, go outside and stand under a real one. We may not fully understand the process of something growing from a small seed to a majestic tree, but we can experience the benefits of that process. Put your hands on the trunk and feel the strength. Bask in the shade of the leaves and branches. Think of the birds, squirrels, and other animals that benefit from the shelter and food the tree provides.

So it is with spiritual growth—we may not always understand the process, but we can still benefit from it, share it, and use it to help ourselves and others connect with their heavenly Father.

THOUGHTS

This space is here for you to jot down some thoughts, write out a prayer, draw a picture, or do whatever you want to help you remember your 10-minute moment.

When I was a kid and would get a hole in the knees of my jeans, Mom didn't take me to get new jeans; she would put a patch on the knee and send me on my way. But those patches never felt like the old jeans did. They were stiff and different—a constant reminder that something wasn't the same. Jesus was trying to do something new, and the religious types were ready to burst and spill their whine… er, wine… everywhere. Jesus' new way didn't fit with their old way of thinking.

2 MINUTES

Read the passage below. Circle or underline any words/phrases/ verses that you feel are important to remember.

Matthew 9:16-17

[16] *"Besides, who would patch old clothing with new cloth? For the new patch would shrink and rip away from the old cloth, leaving an even bigger tear than before.*

[17] *"And no one puts new wine into old wineskins. For the old skins would burst from the pressure, spilling the wine and ruining the skins. New wine is stored in new wineskins so that both are preserved."*

5 MINUTES

Think about the following questions and how they might apply to your life.

- Do you generally like trying new things, or do you generally like things to stay the way they are?
- Why do you think some people are so scared of change?
- If you could change one thing about your relationship with God, what would it be?

3 MINUTES

Hanging out with God

- The key thought here is that the passage says both are preserved. Jesus isn't saying that we have to always have "new wine." He's saying that we can't try to mash together new ways with old ones. That will ruin both paths.
- Ask God to help you be open to new ways of doing things.

THOUGHTS

This space is here for you to jot down some thoughts, write out a prayer, draw a picture, or do whatever you want to help you remember your 10-minute moment.

Have you ever owed anyone anything? Isn't that a terrible feeling? The Bible tells us that the borrower is slave to the lender. That's pretty strong language.

For this parable I'm including some of the verses around it, because it will help you understand the parable better. The woman in this story is called a sinner—this probably means she was a prostitute or someone who slept with many men. Simon—the rules-following Pharisee who had invited Jesus in—can't get past this woman's past. And in doing so, he can't seem to see just *who* is in his house. The woman knows, though, and she finds her sins forgiven—maybe not by those in the town, but by the only one who matters.

2 MINUTES

Read the passage below. Circle or underline any words/phrases/ verses that you feel are important to remember.

Luke 7:36-50

36One of the Pharisees asked Jesus to have dinner with him, so Jesus went to his home and sat down to eat. 37When a certain immoral woman from that city heard he was eating there, she brought a beautiful alabaster jar filled with expensive perfume. 38Then she knelt behind him at his feet, weeping. Her tears fell on his feet, and she wiped them off with her hair. Then she kept kissing his feet and putting perfume on them.

39When the Pharisee who had invited him saw this, he said to himself, "If this man were a prophet, he would know what kind of woman is touching him. She's a sinner!"

⁴⁰Then Jesus answered his thoughts. "Simon," he said to the Pharisee, "I have something to say to you."

"Go ahead, Teacher," Simon replied.

⁴¹Then Jesus told him this story: "A man loaned money to two people—500 pieces of silver to one and 50 pieces to the other. ⁴²But neither of them could repay him, so he kindly forgave them both, canceling their debts. Who do you suppose loved him more after that?"

⁴³Simon answered, "I suppose the one for whom he canceled the larger debt."

"That's right," Jesus said. ⁴⁴Then he turned to the woman and said to Simon, "Look at this woman kneeling here. When I entered your home, you didn't offer me water to wash the dust from my feet, but she has washed them with her tears and wiped them with her hair. ⁴⁵You didn't greet me with a kiss, but from the time I first came in, she has not stopped kissing my feet. ⁴⁶You neglected the courtesy of olive oil to anoint my head, but she has anointed my feet with rare perfume.

⁴⁷"I tell you, her sins—and they are many—have been forgiven, so she has shown me much love. But a person who is forgiven little shows only little love." ⁴⁸Then Jesus said to the woman, "Your sins are forgiven."

⁴⁹The men at the table said among themselves, "Who is this man, that he goes around forgiving sins?"

⁵⁰And Jesus said to the woman, "Your faith has saved you; go in peace."

5 MINUTES

Think about the following questions and how they might apply to your life.
- Why do you think the Pharisee got so mad at the woman's actions?

- Think of an occasion when you found yourself acting like the Pharisee. Why did you do that?
- How do you think Jesus felt as this was happening?
- Do you have a hard time embracing forgiveness? Why or why not?

3 MINUTES

Hanging out with God
- We need to be careful that in following the rules we don't miss the people God has put in our path.
- This account shows us that there's no amount of sin that can't be forgiven. Have you put your trust in God?

EXPERIENCE

If possible, put on a perfume or cologne that you've never worn before—or that you haven't worn in a while. Every time you catch a whiff of it today, think about the beautiful act of the woman toward Jesus, and thank him for his gift of forgiveness.

THOUGHTS

This space is here for you to jot down some thoughts, write out a prayer, draw a picture, or do whatever you want to help you remember your 10-minute moment.

THE SOWER AND THE SOILS

Day 7

This is one of the rare times Jesus explained a parable after telling it. Remember how I told you it was OK that you didn't always understand the parables—that the disciples had trouble, too? Well, Jesus comes right out and explains each of the soils and what they mean.

2 MINUTES

Read the passage below. Circle or underline any words/phrases/verses that you feel are important to remember.

Matthew 13:1-23

[1]Later that same day Jesus left the house and sat beside the lake. [2]A large crowd soon gathered around him, so he got into a boat. Then he sat there and taught as the people stood on the shore. [3]He told many stories in the form of parables, such as this one:

"Listen! A farmer went out to plant some seeds. [4]As he scattered them across his field, some seeds fell on a footpath, and the birds came and ate them. [5]Other seeds fell on shallow soil with underlying rock. The seeds sprouted quickly because the soil was shallow. [6]But the plants soon wilted under the hot sun, and since they didn't have deep roots, they died. [7]Other seeds fell among thorns that grew up and choked out the tender plants. [8]Still other seeds fell on fertile soil, and they produced a crop that was thirty, sixty, and even a hundred times as much as had been planted! [9]Anyone with ears to hear should listen and understand."

¹⁰His disciples came and asked him, "Why do you use parables when you talk to the people?"

¹¹He replied, "You are permitted to understand the secrets of the Kingdom of Heaven, but others are not. ¹²To those who listen to my teaching, more understanding will be given, and they will have an abundance of knowledge. But for those who are not listening, even what little understanding they have will be taken away from them. ¹³That is why I use these parables,

> For they look, but they don't really see. They hear, but they don't really listen or understand.

¹⁴This fulfills the prophecy of Isaiah that says,

> 'When you hear what I say, you will not understand. When you see what I do, you will not comprehend. ¹⁵For the hearts of these people are hardened, and their ears cannot hear, and they have closed their eyes—so their eyes cannot see, and their ears cannot hear, and their hearts cannot understand, and they cannot turn to me and let me heal them.'

¹⁶"But blessed are your eyes, because they see; and your ears, because they hear. ¹⁷I tell you the truth, many prophets and righteous people longed to see what you see, but they didn't see it. And they longed to hear what you hear, but they didn't hear it.

¹⁸"Now listen to the explanation of the parable about the farmer planting seeds: ¹⁹The seed that fell on the footpath represents those who hear the message about the Kingdom and don't understand it. Then the evil one comes and snatches away the seed that was planted in their hearts. ²⁰The seed on the rocky soil represents those who hear the message and immediately receive it with joy. ²¹But since they don't have deep roots, they don't last long. They fall away as soon as they have problems or are persecuted for believing God's word. ²²The seed that fell among the thorns represents those who hear God's word, but all too quickly the message is crowded out by the worries of this life and the lure of wealth, so no fruit is produced. ²³The seed that fell on good soil represents those who truly hear and understand God's word and produce a harvest of thirty, sixty, or even a hundred times as much as had been planted!"

5 MINUTES

Think about the following questions and how they might apply to your life.

- What is required to keep soil healthy? What can keep you healthy?
- Think about the seeds that fell among the weeds. Do you find yourself jealous when something works out "quickly" for someone else? Why or why not? In the same way (and being honest), do you delight when that person "chokes"? Why or why not?
- Look again at the different soils. Consider your own relationship with Christ. Being transparent with God, what soil would describe your life?
- What's one small thing you can do today to get healthier soil in your life? Make a commitment to take that first step today.

3 MINUTES

Hanging out with God

- Ask God to make your heart good soil, where his word can take root.
- What are some ways you can partner with God to help his word take root in the lives of others?

THOUGHTS

This space is here for you to jot down some thoughts, write out a prayer, draw a picture, or do whatever you want to help you remember your 10-minute moment.

Day 8

THE LIGHTED LAMP

Have you ever been camping—or at least way out, away from the city? Didn't the stars seem amazingly brighter than usual? When you don't have all of those city lights casting their constant, dull glow, the stars shine bright. Jesus says that Christians should be shining bright, too. We are the lights in a dark world, and we shouldn't be ashamed to let our light shine brightly. He also calls us salt; in those days salt was used for flavoring, but it was mostly used as a preservative—it kept things from rotting. Are we having a positive effect on those around us? Are we shining bright?

2 MINUTES

Read the passage below. Circle or underline any words/phrases/ verses that you feel are important to remember.

13 "You are the salt of the earth. But what good is salt if it has lost its flavor? Can you make it salty again? It will be thrown out and trampled underfoot as worthless.

14 "You are the light of the world—like a city on a hilltop that cannot be hidden. 15 No one lights a lamp and then puts it under a basket. Instead, a lamp is placed on a stand, where it gives light to everyone in the house. 16 In the same way, let your good deeds shine out for all to see, so that everyone will praise your heavenly Father."

5 MINUTES

Think about the following questions and how they might apply to your life.

- Jesus talks about salt losing its saltiness. What does it look like in real life to lose your "saltiness"?
- What are some ways you can maintain your "saltiness"?
- Think of a time when you chose to "hide your light under a basket." Why did you do that?
- What are some ways you can be salt and light in your world? How willing are you to do those things? Explain.

3 MINUTES

Hanging out with God

- God wants us to shine brightly. Others will know we're truly following God by the light we show. Commit to shining in the dark world, and know that God will be with you every step of the way.

EXPERIENCE

Go to a small room in your home—the bathroom is a great choice—and bring a flashlight. Turn off the lights and close the door so it's dark. Let your eyes adjust. Then point the flashlight at your face and turn it on. Ask yourself: What are all the ways a bright light impacts the darkness?

THOUGHTS

This space is here for you to jot down some thoughts, write out a prayer, draw a picture, or do whatever you want to help you remember your 10-minute moment.

Quick history lesson: The Jews and the Samaritans were enemies. They really, *really* hated each other—and they had for hundreds of years. So what does Jesus do? Just like always, he turns everything upside-down. He tells a story to the Jewish listeners, and makes a Samaritan the hero! "What?! Doesn't Jesus know that we hate those guys?" Of course he does. So maybe this story is about more than just helping out those in need. Just maybe…

2 MINUTES

Read the passage below. Circle or underline any words/phrases/verses that you feel are important to remember.

Luke 10:30-37

³⁰*Jesus replied with a story: "A Jewish man was traveling on a trip from Jerusalem to Jericho, and he was attacked by bandits. They stripped him of his clothes, beat him up, and left him half dead beside the road.*

³¹*"By chance a priest came along. But when he saw the man lying there, he crossed to the other side of the road and passed him by.* ³²*A Temple assistant walked over and looked at him lying there, but he also passed by on the other side.*

³³*"Then a despised Samaritan came along, and when he saw the man, he felt compassion for him.* ³⁴*Going over to him, the Samaritan soothed his wounds with olive oil and wine and bandaged them. Then he put the man on his own donkey and took him to an inn, where he took care of him.* ³⁵*The next day he handed the innkeeper*

two silver coins, telling him, 'Take care of this man. If his bill runs higher than this, I'll pay you the next time I'm here.'

36"Now which of these three would you say was a neighbor to the man who was attacked by bandits?" Jesus asked.

37The man replied, "The one who showed him mercy."

Then Jesus said, "Yes, now go and do the same."

Think about the following questions and how they might apply to your life.
- If Jesus told this story today, who do you think might be in the place of the Samaritan?
- Why do you think Jesus chose one of Israel's "enemies" to be the hero of the story?
- Why did the "good" people pass on the other side of the road?
- Have you ever ignored someone who was in need? Why?
- Have you ever helped someone who might be considered an "enemy"? Why or why not?

Hanging out with God
- Jesus wants us to view and treat everyone—even people we don't like or are uncomfortable with—as our neighbors. Then when we follow his command to love our neighbor as ourselves, we'll have no excuse for not including everyone.
- Ask God to help you be aware of needs as you see them today, and ask God to give you strength to not pass by on the other side of the road.

THOUGHTS

This space is here for you to jot down some thoughts, write out a prayer, draw a picture, or do whatever you want to help you remember your 10-minute moment.

THE RICH FOOL

Day 10

Worry. It's a terrible reality for so many people—and apparently it was a problem for people in Jesus' time, too. "What if I lose my job?" "What if I fail that test?" "What if I don't get into that college?" But here's the truth: When we worry, we act as though we're in control, and not God. Should we study for that test? Absolutely! But if we've done everything we can, what possible good will it do to worry? This man thought he had it all figured out—by himself. But without God, it's just a false sense of security.

2 MINUTES

Read the passage below. Circle or underline any words/phrases/verses that you feel are important to remember.

Luke 12:16-21

[16]*Then he told them a story: "A rich man had a fertile farm that produced fine crops.* [17]*He said to himself, 'What should I do? I don't have room for all my crops.'* [18]*Then he said, 'I know! I'll tear down my barns and build bigger ones. Then I'll have room enough to store all my wheat and other goods.* [19]*And I'll sit back and say to myself, "My friend, you have enough stored away for years to come. Now take it easy! Eat, drink, and be merry!"'*

[20]*"But God said to him, 'You fool! You will die this very night. Then who will get everything you worked for?'*

[21]*"Yes, a person is a fool to store up earthly wealth but not have a rich relationship with God."*

5 MINUTES

Think about the following questions and how they might apply to your life.

- What's the source of the things you worry about the most?
- How does worry impact our relationship with God?
- Do these verses mean we should never prepare for hard times? Why or why not?
- How can we prepare for the future and still trust in God?

3 MINUTES

Hanging out with God

- Think about something that you're worrying about right now. Give that worry to God; trust in him for the outcome—whatever it might be.

THOUGHTS

This space is here for you to jot down some thoughts, write out a prayer, draw a picture, or do whatever you want to help you remember your 10-minute moment.

Day 11

THE FRIEND AT NIGHT

Here we see Jesus comparing God to a homeowner whose friend in need has come to see him. It's interesting that the friend arrives at midnight. Personally, I wouldn't bother a friend in the middle of the night unless it was really important. But Jesus is telling us to be bold with God—with *any* need.

2 MINUTES

Read the passage below. Circle or underline any words/phrases/verses that you feel are important to remember.

Luke 11:5-8

5Then, teaching them more about prayer, he used this story: "Suppose you went to a friend's house at midnight, wanting to borrow three loaves of bread. You say to him, 6'A friend of mine has just arrived for a visit, and I have nothing for him to eat.' 7And suppose he calls out from his bedroom, 'Don't bother me. The door is locked for the night, and my family and I are all in bed. I can't help you.' 8But I tell you this—though he won't do it for friendship's sake, if you keep knocking long enough, he will get up and give you whatever you need because of your shameless persistence."

5 MINUTES

Think about the following questions and how they might apply to your life.

- Do you feel comfortable praying? Why or why not?
- Why would Jesus tell us to "bother" God in prayer?
- Why wouldn't God simply answer our prayers outright?
- What types of things does God care about? How do "everyday things" rank compared to "really important" things—does God treat our prayers differently? Why or why not?

3 MINUTES

Hanging out with God

- Jesus talks about persistence, and persistence requires discipline. Find a time that works well for you, and commit to spending time in prayer every day. Be bold in what you ask for. It may be that God's answer is no, or wait, but don't be afraid of bothering God. He loves spending time with us.

EXPERIENCE

Consider making a prayer journal. Nothing fancy—just something that's yours. When you pray about something, write it down in the journal along with the date. Then track the prayers as God answers them. Some prayers may take a long time to be answered, but seeing that God was at work all along is an amazing sight!

THOUGHTS

This space is here for you to jot down some thoughts, write out a prayer, draw a picture, or do whatever you want to help you remember your 10-minute moment.

THE BARREN FIG TREE

Day 12

When you're in a harsh, desert region—like Jerusalem—water is a precious thing. And when you have a tree that's not producing fruit, well, that's just wasting water, space, and time. In this parable, the vineyard owner represents God, and he's wondering why there's no fruit on the tree. The gardener represents Jesus, and he's asking God the Father to give him some time to produce some fruit. If the tree still won't produce after the gardener's work, then it can be thrown out. We have to ask ourselves if we're producing fruit. If we're not, what will become of us?

2 MINUTES

Read the passage below. Circle or underline any words/phrases/verses that you feel are important to remember.

Luke 13:6-9

⁶Then Jesus told this story: "A man planted a fig tree in his garden and came again and again to see if there was any fruit on it, but he was always disappointed. ⁷Finally, he said to his gardener, 'I've waited three years, and there hasn't been a single fig! Cut it down. It's just taking up space in the garden.'

⁸"The gardener answered, 'Sir, give it one more chance. Leave it another year, and I'll give it special attention and plenty of fertilizer. ⁹If we get figs next year, fine. If not, then you can cut it down.'"

5 MINUTES

Think about the following questions and how they might apply to your life.

- What do you hope Jesus is "interceding" for you before his Father? Explain?
- What does it look like to produce fruit for God's kingdom?
- In what areas of your life are you producing fruit?
- What's an area that you're feeling needs more "fertilizer"?

3 MINUTES

Hanging out with God

- Ask God to point out any areas of your life that aren't producing fruit.
- Commit to God that you will heed his call to be fruitful. Ultimately, we can't create fruit on our own, but we must be open to God working in our lives before the fruit will come.
- Take a piece of fruit with you for lunch this week. As you eat that fruit, ask God to point out areas in your life where you need to bear more fruit. Then commit to working on those areas with God's help.

THOUGHTS

This space is here for you to jot down some thoughts, write out a prayer, draw a picture, or do whatever you want to help you remember your 10-minute moment.

THE MUSTARD SEED AND LEAVEN

Day 13

Think back to the time you were *really* sick. It's not a pleasant memory, I'm sure. But what's amazing is how much something as small as a germ can affect our lives. You can't even see germs with the naked eye, but they'll put you out of commission for days at a time! The people of Jesus' time didn't know anything about germs, but they did know about seeds. A mustard seed is really small, but it produces a really large tree. And similarly, a small amount of leaven can work through a batch of bread and help it rise. Small acts can have big results.

2 MINUTES

Read the passage below. Circle or underline any words/phrases/verses that you feel are important to remember.

Luke 13:18-21

¹⁸*Then Jesus said, "What is the Kingdom of God like? How can I illustrate it? ¹⁹It is like a tiny mustard seed that a man planted in a garden; it grows and becomes a tree, and the birds make nests in its branches."*

²⁰*He also asked, "What else is the Kingdom of God like? ²¹It is like the yeast a woman used in making bread. Even though she put only a little yeast in three measures of flour, it permeated every part of the dough."*

5 MINUTES

Think about the following questions and how they might apply to your life.

- Why would Jesus compare the kingdom of God to such small things?
- One small drip of water—over enough time—could carve another Grand Canyon. What's a small thing you've been doing that's produced big results? Explain.
- What does it take to turn a tiny mustard seed into an enormous tree? In what area of your life do you need God's miraculous touch?

3 MINUTES

Hanging out with God

- Every small, good action can have an eternal impact. Pray for an opportunity to do a small action, every day, for God and his kingdom.

THOUGHTS

This space is here for you to jot down some thoughts, write out a prayer, draw a picture, or do whatever you want to help you remember your 10-minute moment.

THE GREAT BANQUET

Day 14

This is a strange parable. Most parables find Jesus using seemingly unrelated examples to tell us about the kingdom of God. But this parable seems uncharacteristically straightforward. "Take care of the poor," Jesus says. "Yes, but what do you mean by that, Jesus?" we ask. We're looking for hidden meaning, but there is none. Take care of the poor—those people on the fringes, who don't normally get invited to the big parties. Jesus came for them, too. And when the poor and hungry are missing from our church buildings, something's not right.

2 MINUTES

Read the passage below. Circle or underline any words/phrases/ verses that you feel are important to remember.

Luke 14:16-24

16Jesus replied with this story: "A man prepared a great feast and sent out many invitations. 17When the banquet was ready, he sent his servant to tell the guests, 'Come, the banquet is ready.' 18But they all began making excuses. One said, 'I have just bought a field and must inspect it. Please excuse me.' 19Another said, 'I have just bought five pairs of oxen, and I want to try them out. Please excuse me.' 20Another said, 'I now have a wife, so I can't come.'

21"The servant returned and told his master what they had said. His master was furious and said, 'Go quickly into the streets and alleys of the town and invite the poor, the crippled, the blind, and the lame.' 22After the servant had done this, he reported, 'There is still room for more.' 23So his master said, 'Go out into the country lanes and behind the hedges and urge anyone you find to come, so that the house will be full. ²⁴For none of those I first invited will get even the smallest taste of my banquet.'"

5 MINUTES

Think about the following questions and how they might apply to your life.
- Why do you think Jesus had such concern for the poor?
- Why do the poor, crippled, blind, and lame make people so uncomfortable?
- What are some of the excuses "well" people give for missing the banquet?

3 MINUTES

Hanging out with God
- It's obvious God has a heart for the poor. If we're to have a heart like God, we should have a heart for them, too. What does that look like for you personally? What does that look like for your youth group? What does that look like for your city? How would a heart change like that make God feel? Ask him.

EXPERIENCE

Take a handful of snacks—granola bars or fruit—to school. Then, during the passing period between classes, offer your snacks to the students passing by you in the hallway. As you hand the snack to someone, silently pray for him or her.

THOUGHTS

This space is here for you to jot down some thoughts, write out a prayer, draw a picture, or do whatever you want to help you remember your 10-minute moment.

At first glance, this is one of the oddest passages in the Bible. "Is Jesus *really* saying that if I want to follow him, I have to hate my family?" Well… no. Jesus is saying that following him won't be easy. In fact, it might cost you everything—your possessions, your family, and your life. Dietrich Bonhoeffer was a German pastor and a participant in the resistance against the Nazis who was imprisoned by the Nazis during World War II. He never got out of jail, but before he was killed, he wrote some amazing books on what it costs to follow Jesus. And it cost Bonhoeffer his life—he understood these passages. We may not have to give it all up, but true discipleship means we're willing to.

2 MINUTES

Read the passage below. Circle or underline any words/phrases/ verses that you feel are important to remember.

Luke 14:28-33

[28] "But don't begin until you count the cost. For who would begin construction of a building without first calculating the cost to see if there is enough money to finish it? [29]Otherwise, you might complete only the foundation before running out of money, and then everyone would laugh at you. [30]They would say, 'There's the person who started that building and couldn't afford to finish it!'

[31] "Or what king would go to war against another king without first sitting down with his counselors to discuss whether his army of 10,000 could defeat the 20,000 soldiers marching against him? [32]And if he can't, he will send a delegation to discuss terms of

peace while the enemy is still far away. [33]So you cannot become my disciple without giving up everything you own."

5 MINUTES

Think about the following questions and how they might apply to your life.
- What is your initial reaction to Jesus' words here?
- When have you started something you couldn't finish? What did you learn from that experience?
- Reflect on what's important to you. How do you spend your time? Your money? If you only looked at your time and money, what would you conclude are your life's priorities?

3 MINUTES

Hanging out with God
- God might not ask you to give up everything you own, but he wants to know that we're willing to. Spend the next three minutes talking to God about where you are right now. It's OK if this is hard or if you're not ready. Talk to God about it. He'd love to hear from you.

THOUGHTS

This space is here for you to jot down some thoughts, write out a prayer, draw a picture, or do whatever you want to help you remember your 10-minute moment.

I hate weeds. I really, really do. First, they're *everywhere*. Second, they're really hard to kill. And third, as soon as you do kill one, it seems that three take its place. But our first instinct when we see a weed is to just pull it. Of course, Jesus isn't talking about weeds here. He's talking about us. God has planted "wheat"—his righteousness—in us. But we often still struggle with the "weeds" our "enemy" has sown in our life. We're tempted to work hard to pull up those weeds, but this parable challenges that conventional wisdom.

2 MINUTES

Read the passage below. Circle or underline any words/phrases/verses that you feel are important to remember.

Matthew 13:24-30

²⁴Here is another story Jesus told: "The Kingdom of Heaven is like a farmer who planted good seed in his field. ²⁵But that night as the workers slept, his enemy came and planted weeds among the wheat, then slipped away. ²⁶When the crop began to grow and produce grain, the weeds also grew.

²⁷"The farmer's workers went to him and said, 'Sir, the field where you planted that good seed is full of weeds! Where did they come from?'

²⁸"'An enemy has done this!' the farmer exclaimed.

"'Should we pull out the weeds?' they asked.

29"'No,' he replied, 'you'll uproot the wheat if you do. 30Let both grow together until the harvest. Then I will tell the harvesters to sort out the weeds, tie them into bundles, and burn them, and to put the wheat in the barn.'"

Think about the following questions and how they might apply to your life.
- What are some "weeds" in your life right now? If you followed the wisdom of this parable, what is God asking you to do about those weeds?
- How can we be sure we're not being weeds?

Hanging out with God
- God is willing to let the weeds grow with the wheat, but he assures us the day will come when the two will be separated— one to the storehouses, and the other to be burned.
- Talk to God about how much you want to be wheat and what steps are necessary to do that.

Sit in a lawn somewhere—at home, in a park, or even at school. Spend a few minutes looking for weeds in the lawn and attempting to pull them up without affecting the grass. Ask God: "Specifically, what are you teaching me right now through this parable?"

THOUGHTS

This space is here for you to jot down some thoughts, write out a prayer, draw a picture, or do whatever you want to help you remember your 10-minute moment.

Jesus is often portrayed as just a nice, wise teacher—and he is that, of course. But he was about very serious business. As he got closer to the end of his life, he started talking more and more about that serious business. There are only two choices in life: You're either a good fish or a bad fish. It's as simple and as complex as that. Have you ever smelled bad fish? I'm not sure there's a worse smell—OK, maybe the boys' cabin at a junior high retreat.

Read the passage below. Circle or underline any words/phrases/ verses that you feel are important to remember.

Matthew 13:47-50
47"Again, the Kingdom of Heaven is like a fishing net that was thrown into the water and caught fish of every kind. 48When the net was full, they dragged it up onto the shore, sat down, and sorted the good fish into crates, but threw the bad ones away. 49That is the way it will be at the end of the world. The angels will come and separate the wicked people from the righteous, 50throwing the wicked into the fiery furnace, where there will be weeping and gnashing of teeth."

5 MINUTES

Think about the following questions and how they might apply to your life.

- How do you know whether or not you're a "good fish" or a "bad fish"?
- What does it mean that "bad fish" made it into the net at all?
- The bad fish here seem to be people who heard the gospel and dismissed it. What are some reasons people give for dismissing the good news of Jesus?

3 MINUTES

Hanging out with God

- You've heard the good news, and you can choose to be a good fish. It's important—in fact, there's nothing more important in the entire world. Spend time committing to be a good fish for God.

THOUGHTS

This space is here for you to jot down some thoughts, write out a prayer, draw a picture, or do whatever you want to help you remember your 10-minute moment.

For years, every time I read these passages, I assumed it was about someone who discovers the great worth of a life with Christ and decides to give up everything for him. But I'm not so sure that's right, anymore. What if the man and merchant in these parables represent Jesus? And what if we are the thing of great worth he gives up everything to purchase—with his life.

2 MINUTES

Read the passage below. Circle or underline any words/phrases/verses that you feel are important to remember.

Matthew 13:44-46

[44]*"The Kingdom of Heaven is like a treasure that a man discovered hidden in a field. In his excitement, he hid it again and sold everything he owned to get enough money to buy the field.*

[45]*"Again, the Kingdom of Heaven is like a merchant on the lookout for choice pearls.* [46]*When he discovered a pearl of great value, he sold everything he owned and bought it!"*

5 MINUTES

Think about the following questions and how they might apply to your life.

- What's the central truth buried in these parables?
- Have you ever loved anything enough to give up everything for it?
- Why would Jesus give up everything for us?
- Do you think we owe him anything for that gift? Explain.
- What are you already doing in your life to thank Jesus for that gift?

3 MINUTES

Hanging out with God
- Thank God for the gift of his son—and for loving us as much as he does.

EXPERIENCE

Pull the classifieds section out of a newspaper. Think about everything you own, and how much it would be worth if you sold it all. Now see if you can find something in the classifieds that you'd be willing to sell everything to get. What new insights do you have about this parable now?

THOUGHTS

This space is here for you to jot down some thoughts, write out a prayer, draw a picture, or do whatever you want to help you remember your 10-minute moment.

THE UNFORGIVING SERVANT

Day 19

When you put your faith in Jesus, all of your sins are forgiven. In an instant, it's as though it never happened. Some of us have many things to be forgiven of, and some have only a few things—but we're *all* sinners, and we all need forgiveness. Sometimes, though, we treat others as though we've forgotten all that God has done for us. How can I be angry at someone when the death sentence that was upon me is only gone because of God's grace? Shouldn't I show that same grace to those who have wronged me, or who "owe" me?

2 MINUTES

Read the passage below. Circle or underline any words/phrases/verses that you feel are important to remember.

Matthew 18:21-35

21 Then Peter came to him and asked, "Lord, how often should I forgive someone who sins against me? Seven times?"

22 "No, not seven times," Jesus replied, "but seventy times seven!

23 "Therefore, the Kingdom of Heaven can be compared to a king who decided to bring his accounts up to date with servants who had borrowed money from him. 24 In the process, one of his debtors was brought in who owed him millions of dollars. 25 He couldn't pay, so his master ordered that he be sold—along with his wife, his children, and everything he owned—to pay the debt.

26 "But the man fell down before his master and begged him, 'Please, be patient with me, and I will pay it all.' 27 Then his master was filled with pity for him, and he released him and forgave his debt.

[28]"But when the man left the king, he went to a fellow servant who owed him a few thousand dollars. He grabbed him by the throat and demanded instant payment.

[29]"His fellow servant fell down before him and begged for a little more time. 'Be patient with me, and I will pay it,' he pleaded. [30]But his creditor wouldn't wait. He had the man arrested and put in prison until the debt could be paid in full.

[31]"When some of the other servants saw this, they were very upset. They went to the king and told him everything that had happened. [32]Then the king called in the man he had forgiven and said, 'You evil servant! I forgave you that tremendous debt because you pleaded with me. [33]Shouldn't you have mercy on your fellow servant, just as I had mercy on you?' [34]Then the angry king sent the man to prison to be tortured until he had paid his entire debt.

[35]"That's what my heavenly Father will do to you if you refuse to forgive your brothers and sisters from your heart."

5 MINUTES

Think about the following questions and how they might apply to your life.
- When have you forgiven someone of an offense against you?
- How did you feel afterward?
- Why do people find it so hard to forgive?
- Because it's so hard to forgive, there's great power in it—great freedom in it. Is there anyone you need to forgive—even if that person hasn't asked for it or apologized?
- What is keeping you from forgiving that person?

3 MINUTES

Hanging out with God
- When I stop and remember just what God has done for me, it makes me see other people as he sees them—when that happens, the world gets brighter, lovelier, and more achingly beautiful.

THOUGHTS

This space is here for you to jot down some thoughts, write out a prayer, draw a picture, or do whatever you want to help you remember your 10-minute moment.

Day 20

THE RICH MAN AND LAZARUS

Here we have another teaching about how we should treat the poor. So many people want to ignore them and forget them and just hope they'll go away. It seems harsh that when the rich man asks that Lazarus be sent to warn the rich man's brothers, the request is denied. But Jesus is warning those who were listening then—and are listening now—that they should be prepared for the kingdom that is coming. And knowing what would happen to Jesus in a short time, his words "they won't listen even if someone rises from the dead" add another layer of meaning.

2 MINUTES

Read the passage below. Circle or underline any words/phrases/verses that you feel are important to remember.

Luke 16:19-31

¹⁹Jesus said, "There was a certain rich man who was splendidly clothed in purple and fine linen and who lived each day in luxury. ²⁰At his gate lay a poor man named Lazarus who was covered with sores. ²¹As Lazarus lay there longing for scraps from the rich man's table, the dogs would come and lick his open sores.

²²"Finally, the poor man died and was carried by the angels to be with Abraham. The rich man also died and was buried, ²³and his soul went to the place of the dead. There, in torment, he saw Abraham in the far distance with Lazarus at his side.

²⁴"The rich man shouted, 'Father Abraham, have some pity! Send Lazarus over here to dip the tip of his finger in water and cool my tongue. I am in anguish in these flames.'

²⁵ *"But Abraham said to him, 'Son, remember that during your lifetime you had everything you wanted, and Lazarus had nothing. So now he is here being comforted, and you are in anguish. ²⁶ And besides, there is a great chasm separating us. No one can cross over to you from here, and no one can cross over to us from there.'*

²⁷ *"Then the rich man said, 'Please, Father Abraham, at least send him to my father's home. ²⁸ For I have five brothers, and I want him to warn them so they don't end up in this place of torment.'*

²⁹ *"But Abraham said, 'Moses and the prophets have warned them. Your brothers can read what they wrote.'*

³⁰ *"The rich man replied, 'No, Father Abraham! But if someone is sent to them from the dead, then they will repent of their sins and turn to God.'*

³¹ *"But Abraham said, 'If they won't listen to Moses and the prophets, they won't listen even if someone rises from the dead.'"*

5 MINUTES

Think about the following questions and how they might apply to your life.
- Do you think the rich man is in the "place of torment" because of his treatment of the poor? Why or why not?
- This parable seems to have a sense of urgency about it. Why would Jesus make such an urgent plea for the poor when he was trying to bring people to the Father?

3 MINUTES

Hanging out with God
- What are some things you could donate to a thrift store or homeless shelter—things that you rarely use, or things that could be put to greater use by someone in need? Challenge yourself to look for opportunities to give to those less fortunate. You could even ask your family to do the same.

- Take a few minutes to thank God for the blessings he's given you and your family, and ask him to help you be aware of needs that pop up around you.

THOUGHTS

This space is here for you to jot down some thoughts, write out a prayer, draw a picture, or do whatever you want to help you remember your 10-minute moment.

Day 21

THE MASTER AND SERVANT

Humility is something we don't often get a chance to practice. Jesus seemingly says, "The things you do, I want you to do them because I ask you to, and not because you'll get any kind of recognition. Remember, there is a God, and you're not him."

2 MINUTES

Read the passage below. Circle or underline any words/phrases/verses that you feel are important to remember.

Luke 17:7-10

[7] *"When a servant comes in from plowing or taking care of sheep, does his master say, 'Come in and eat with me'?* [8] *No, he says, 'Prepare my meal, put on your apron, and serve me while I eat. Then you can eat later.'* [9] *And does the master thank the servant for doing what he was told to do? Of course not.* [10] *In the same way, when you obey me you should say, 'We are unworthy servants who have simply done our duty.'"*

5 MINUTES

Think about the following questions and how they might apply to your life.

- If you had to convey the "essence" of this parable to someone who's never read the Bible, what would you say?
- Why is our obedience such a big deal to God?
- Do these verses mean we're slaves? Why or why not?
- How can we "prepare" something for God to eat? What does that look like?

3 MINUTES

Hanging out with God

- If you've been obeying God out of a desire for recognition, ask his forgiveness.
- Commit to serving God out of love and a right view of our place in his universe, and not a desire for recognition.

EXPERIENCE

Find a place where you can be quiet and uninterrupted for a few minutes. Then ask God to show you one thing you can do for him today out of simple obedience—something you're not likely to be recognized or rewarded for. Then go do it.

THOUGHTS

This space is here for you to jot down some thoughts, write out a prayer, draw a picture, or do whatever you want to help you remember your 10-minute moment.

There are few things more surprising than a rotten person doing the right thing. I think that's why it happens so often in movies—it surprises us, and surprises make for good storytelling. So here we have a judge who seems to be a rotten guy—he doesn't fear God, and he doesn't respect people. How did he get to be a judge, anyway? So a woman wants him to help her out, and he's not really interested, but her persistence wears him down, and he finally agrees. How much more will the completely not-rotten God give us justice when we ask?

2 MINUTES

Read the passage below. Circle or underline any words/phrases/ verses that you feel are important to remember.

Luke 18:1-8

¹One day Jesus told his disciples a story to show that they should always pray and never give up. ²"There was a judge in a certain city," he said, "who neither feared God nor cared about people. ³A widow of that city came to him repeatedly, saying, 'Give me justice in this dispute with my enemy.' ⁴The judge ignored her for a while, but finally he said to himself, 'I don't fear God or care about people, ⁵but this woman is driving me crazy. I'm going to see that she gets justice, because she is wearing me out with her constant requests!'"

⁶Then the Lord said, "Learn a lesson from this unjust judge. ⁷Even he rendered a just decision in the end. So don't you think God will surely give justice to his chosen people who cry out to him day and night? Will he keep putting them off? ⁸I tell you, he will grant justice to them quickly! But when the Son of Man returns, how many will he find on the earth who have faith?"

Think about the following questions and how they might apply to your life.

- This parable seems to assume we're before some sort of judge. What is the lawsuit about?
- Have you ever gone to God over and over with the same request? How did you feel doing that?
- God is the ultimate authority; he is Justice. Is it easy or hard to trust God and his decisions? Explain.

Hanging out with God

- If there's something you're seeking an answer on, give it to God, and then let him have it. Be prepared for an answer of no, or an answer of wait, or an answer of yes. But trust that God loves you and cares about your needs. He is a just judge.

THOUGHTS

This space is here for you to jot down some thoughts, write out a prayer, draw a picture, or do whatever you want to help you remember your 10-minute moment.

Day 23

THE PHARISEES AND THE PUBLICAN

Have you ever compared yourself to someone else? We do that a lot, don't we? Sometimes we do it to make ourselves feel better or look better—often to justify our actions. "Well, I may have done X, but at least I don't do Y, like that guy does." It shows contempt for God—like he's a divine bookkeeper, comparing our sins against others.

2 MINUTES

Read the passage below. Circle or underline any words/phrases/ verses that you feel are important to remember.

Luke 18:9-14

⁹Then Jesus told this story to some who had great confidence in their own righteousness and scorned everyone else: ¹⁰"Two men went to the Temple to pray. One was a Pharisee, and the other was a despised tax collector. ¹¹The Pharisee stood by himself and prayed this prayer: 'I thank you, God, that I am not a sinner like everyone else. For I don't cheat, I don't sin, and I don't commit adultery. I'm certainly not like that tax collector! ¹²I fast twice a week, and I give you a tenth of my income.'

¹³"But the tax collector stood at a distance and dared not even lift his eyes to heaven as he prayed. Instead, he beat his chest in sorrow, saying, 'O God, be merciful to me, for I am a sinner.' ¹⁴I tell you, this sinner, not the Pharisee, returned home justified before God. For those who exalt themselves will be humbled, and those who humble themselves will be exalted."

5 MINUTES

Think about the following questions and how they might apply to your life.

- Think about a time you tried to exalt yourself by talking about someone else's faults. How did you feel afterward?
- The prayer of the tax collector seems so genuine, heartfelt, and powerful. He can't even look up at heaven. When have you prayed a desperate, simple prayer like the tax collector's?
- If you've never prayed this way, why do you think that is?

3 MINUTES

Hanging out with God

- The word "justified" that Jesus uses means that he was absolved—acquitted. Notice that the Pharisee follows the "rules" (tithing, fasting, and so forth), but Jesus says that the man who shows a great and simple faith is the one who goes home justified.
- Repent of times when you've compared yourself to others. Come to God now, just as you are, and talk to him. It's about you and God, and no one else.

THOUGHTS

This space is here for you to jot down some thoughts, write out a prayer, draw a picture, or do whatever you want to help you remember your 10-minute moment.

THE WORKERS IN THE VINEYARD

"That's not fair!" Have you ever said that? I have. The workers in this parable that get so upset agreed to a certain amount of work for a certain amount of pay. So why did they end up getting upset? We want God to be so generous to us, but we get huffy when he's generous to other people. This is rooted in selfishness—when we start to wrongly think it's all about us. It isn't.

2 MINUTES

Read the passage below. Circle or underline any words/phrases/ verses that you feel are important to remember.

Matthew 20:1-16

¹"For the Kingdom of Heaven is like the landowner who went out early one morning to hire workers for his vineyard. ²He agreed to pay the normal daily wage and sent them out to work.

³"At nine o'clock in the morning he was passing through the marketplace and saw some people standing around doing nothing. ⁴So he hired them, telling them he would pay them whatever was right at the end of the day. ⁵So they went to work in the vineyard. At noon and again at three o'clock he did the same thing.

⁶"At five o'clock that afternoon he was in town again and saw some more people standing around. He asked them, 'Why haven't you been working today?'

⁷"They replied, 'Because no one hired us.'

"The landowner told them, 'Then go out and join the others in my vineyard.'

[8]"That evening he told the foreman to call the workers in and pay them, beginning with the last workers first. [9]When those hired at five o'clock were paid, each received a full day's wage. [10]When those hired first came to get their pay, they assumed they would receive more. But they, too, were paid a day's wage. [11]When they received their pay, they protested to the owner, [12]'Those people worked only one hour, and yet you've paid them just as much as you paid us who worked all day in the scorching heat.'

[13]"He answered one of them, 'Friend, I haven't been unfair! Didn't you agree to work all day for the usual wage? [14]Take your money and go. I wanted to pay this last worker the same as you. [15]Is it against the law for me to do what I want with my money? Should you be jealous because I am kind to others?'

[16]"So those who are last now will be first then, and those who are first will be last."

5 MINUTES

Think about the following questions and how they might apply to your life.
- Do you empathize with why the workers got so upset? Why or why not?
- Why do you think the landowner wouldn't give those who had worked longer more money?
- Where do we get our ideas of what's "fair" and what isn't?
- Why do God's view of fairness and our view differ sometimes?

3 MINUTES

Hanging out with God
- Seeing the world as unfair is really about selfishness. The only way to really get rid of selfishness is to give ourselves to God. Pray that God would take your selfishness, and that he'd help you start to see others as he does.

EXPERIENCE

Get a small notebook and keep it with you at all times. Every time you say or think the words, "That's not fair," write it in book—where you were, when it happened, what the circumstances were, and so on. After a week, go over each of the incidents and think about the fairness of the circumstance. Was it really unfair? Was it just unfair to you? Could it be that it was fair to someone else, and God was blessing that person? Pray that God would help you think less about whether something's fair, and more about whether it's right—and not just right for you.

THOUGHTS

This space is here for you to jot down some thoughts, write out a prayer, draw a picture, or do whatever you want to help you remember your 10-minute moment.

THE TWO SONS

Repentance. It's kind of a "churchy" word, but I want you to understand how powerful it is, so it stops being churchy and starts being beautiful. The word "repent" means "to turn back." We've sinned, which means we're no longer moving toward God. But when we repent, we understand what we've done, and we turn back to him and begin moving toward him again.

Read the passage below. Circle or underline any words/phrases/ verses that you feel are important to remember.

Matthew 21:28-32
28 "But what do you think about this? A man with two sons told the older boy, 'Son, go out and work in the vineyard today.' 29 The son answered, 'No, I won't go,' but later he changed his mind and went anyway. 30 Then the father told the other son, 'You go,' and he said, 'Yes, sir, I will.' But he didn't go.

31 "Which of the two obeyed his father?"

They replied, "The first."

Then Jesus explained his meaning: "I tell you the truth, corrupt tax collectors and prostitutes will get into the Kingdom of God before you do. 32 For John the Baptist came and showed you the right way to live, but you didn't believe him, while tax collectors and prostitutes did. And even when you saw this happening, you refused to believe him and repent of your sins."

5 MINUTES

Think about the following questions and how they might apply to your life.

- Notice that the son who ultimately does the father's will doesn't want to at first. But he regrets it—repents—and goes to do his father's bidding. Think of a time you chose not to do something when you knew God wanted you to. Why did you make that choice?
- Did you eventually do the right thing? Why or why not?
- What do these verses tell us about giving God "lip service"— telling him we trust and believe him but not following through?

3 MINUTES

Hanging out with God

- Spend the next three minutes asking God to show you any areas where you've been disobedient. Then turn back to God, and do his will. He'll be with you the whole way.

THOUGHTS

This space is here for you to jot down some thoughts, write out a prayer, draw a picture, or do whatever you want to help you remember your 10-minute moment.

Day 26

THE TENANTS

At this point Jesus is coming to the end of his ministry on earth. So many of his parables seem more serious and more about his death and eventual return. The earlier ones dealt with that, too, but in a less obvious way. This one, for instance, comes right out and says that God has sent others who were killed, and now he's sent his son, who will also be killed. But Jesus also reveals that he's the cornerstone, the most important piece in the construction of a building—the one that everything else is built on.

2 MINUTES

Read the passage below. Circle or underline any words/phrases/ verses that you feel are important to remember.

Luke 20:9-16

⁹Now Jesus turned to the people again and told them this story: "A man planted a vineyard, leased it to tenant farmers, and moved to another country to live for several years. ¹⁰At the time of the grape harvest, he sent one of his servants to collect his share of the crop. But the farmers attacked the servant, beat him up, and sent him back empty-handed. ¹¹So the owner sent another servant, but they also insulted him, beat him up, and sent him away empty-handed. ¹²A third man was sent, and they wounded him and chased him away.

¹³"'What will I do?' the owner asked himself. 'I know! I'll send my cherished son. Surely they will respect him.'

14 "But when the tenant farmers saw his son, they said to each other, 'Here comes the heir to this estate. Let's kill him and get the estate for ourselves!' *15* So they dragged him out of the vineyard and murdered him.

"What do you suppose the owner of the vineyard will do to them?" Jesus asked. *16* "I'll tell you—he will come and kill those farmers and lease the vineyard to others."

"How terrible that such a thing should ever happen," his listeners protested.

5 MINUTES

Think about the following questions and how they might apply to your life.
- Why do you think the earlier workers, and then Jesus, were killed?
- Have you ever considered yourself a "tenant"? What are some things that are true of tenants that can apply to us?
- Jesus says that everyone who falls on the stone will be broken to pieces. Why would that be a good thing?

3 MINUTES

Hanging out with God
- God isn't done sending people to tell of the coming of the kingdom. Every day, people choose to proclaim the good news of Jesus. Consider becoming someone who tells people about the glorious things God has done.

THOUGHTS

This space is here for you to jot down some thoughts, write out a prayer, draw a picture, or do whatever you want to help you remember your 10-minute moment.

THE PRODIGAL SON

This is easily my favorite parable. It's full of powerful images: of the reconciliation of a father and the son he loves. A brother who can't be happy at the return of his selfish brother. A selfish guy who ends up fighting pigs for food! But I think my favorite image is that of a father running—*running!*—to greet his lost son, the one he's been looking for every day since he left. And to think, that love is nothing compared to the love God has for us, and the joy he feels when we return to him.

2 MINUTES

Read the passage below. Circle or underline any words/phrases/verses that you feel are important to remember.

Luke 15:11-32

11To illustrate the point further, Jesus told them this story: "A man had two sons. 12The younger son told his father, 'I want my share of your estate now before you die.' So his father agreed to divide his wealth between his sons.

13"A few days later this younger son packed all his belongings and moved to a distant land, and there he wasted all his money in wild living. 14About the time his money ran out, a great famine swept over the land, and he began to starve. 15He persuaded a local farmer to hire him, and the man sent him into his fields to feed the pigs. 16The young man became so hungry that even the pods he was feeding the pigs looked good to him. But no one gave him anything.

¹⁷"When he finally came to his senses, he said to himself, 'At home even the hired servants have food enough to spare, and here I am dying of hunger! ¹⁸I will go home to my father and say, "Father, I have sinned against both heaven and you, ¹⁹and I am no longer worthy of being called your son. Please take me on as a hired servant."'

²⁰"So he returned home to his father. And while he was still a long way off, his father saw him coming. Filled with love and compassion, he ran to his son, embraced him, and kissed him. ²¹His son said to him, 'Father, I have sinned against both heaven and you, and I am no longer worthy of being called your son.'

²²"But his father said to the servants, 'Quick! Bring the finest robe in the house and put it on him. Get a ring for his finger and sandals for his feet. ²³And kill the calf we have been fattening. We must celebrate with a feast, ²⁴for this son of mine was dead and has now returned to life. He was lost, but now he is found.' So the party began.

²⁵"Meanwhile, the older son was in the fields working. When he returned home, he heard music and dancing in the house, ²⁶and he asked one of the servants what was going on. ²⁷'Your brother is back,' he was told, 'and your father has killed the fattened calf. We are celebrating because of his safe return.'

²⁸"The older brother was angry and wouldn't go in. His father came out and begged him, ²⁹but he replied, 'All these years I've slaved for you and never once refused to do a single thing you told me to. And in all that time you never gave me even one young goat for a feast with my friends. ³⁰Yet when this son of yours comes back after squandering your money on prostitutes, you celebrate by killing the fattened calf!'

³¹"His father said to him, 'Look, dear son, you have always stayed by me, and everything I have is yours. ³²We had to celebrate this happy day. For your brother was dead and has come back to life! He was lost, but now he is found!'"

5 MINUTES

Think about the following questions and how they might apply to your life.

- Have you ever felt like running away from it all like the first brother did? What caused that feeling? What did you decide to do, and why?
- When have you had to apologize to your parents for your behavior?
- Have you ever felt like the older brother does in this story? Explain.
- If you were the father, how would you have reacted to the younger son's request for his share of the inheritance?
- Which son in the story was "harder to reach," and why?
- What does this story teach us about our relationship with God?

3 MINUTES

Hanging out with God

- Picture God running with his arms outstretched to greet you. How does that make you feel? Thank him for loving you that much.

EXPERIENCE

When we read this parable, it's easy to identify ourselves with the younger son and the older son, but we don't often put ourselves in the shoes of the father. Today, think of someone who has hurt you, then decide on a way to offer that person a small gift of love—it could be a hug, a card, a poke on Facebook™, and so on.

THOUGHTS

This space is here for you to jot down some thoughts, write out a prayer, draw a picture, or do whatever you want to help you remember your 10-minute moment.

THE BUDDING FIG TREE

This is the second parable Jesus tells about a fig tree. But this time the tree is budding. The budding tree here tells us that summer is near. Jesus is using that imagery to discuss the coming kingdom of God. You can see the effects of the sun—and the Son—and know that a change is coming. We have to be ready with the message—there's nothing more important.

2 MINUTES

Read the passage below. Circle or underline any words/phrases/verses that you feel are important to remember.

Luke 21:29-33

²⁹Then he gave them this illustration: "Notice the fig tree, or any other tree. ³⁰When the leaves come out, you know without being told that summer is near. ³¹In the same way, when you see all these things taking place, you can know that the Kingdom of God is near. ³²I tell you the truth, this generation will not pass from the scene until all these things have taken place. ³³Heaven and earth will disappear, but my words will never disappear."

5 MINUTES

Think about the following questions and how they might apply to your life.

- How do you understand what the "kingdom of God" really is?
- What is different, and what is the same, in the "kingdom of God"?
- What's evidence of the "kingdom of God" in your life?

3 MINUTES

Hanging out with God

- These verses reveal that the kingdom of God is coming near. What better way to be prepared for that coming than to constantly connect with God himself?
- Make connecting with God your number one priority. When that's number one, everything else will seem less pressing, less important.

THOUGHTS

This space is here for you to jot down some thoughts, write out a prayer, draw a picture, or do whatever you want to help you remember your 10-minute moment.

THE FAITHFUL SERVANT

No one likes a pop quiz… well, except the teachers. But even "pop" quizzes aren't really bad, are they? Unless you didn't read the assignment. If you do the work you're supposed to, no pop quiz will ever faze you. It's when we aren't paying attention that we become fearful and unprepared. I want my heart and mind to be prepared for Jesus' arrival, don't you?

Read the passage below. Circle or underline any words/phrases/verses that you feel are important to remember.

Luke 12:35-48

35 "Be dressed for service and keep your lamps burning, 36 as though you were waiting for your master to return from the wedding feast. Then you will be ready to open the door and let him in the moment he arrives and knocks. 37 The servants who are ready and waiting for his return will be rewarded. I tell you the truth, he himself will seat them, put on an apron, and serve them as they sit and eat! 38 He may come in the middle of the night or just before dawn. But whenever he comes, he will reward the servants who are ready.

39 "Understand this: If a homeowner knew exactly when a burglar was coming, he would not permit his house to be broken into. 40 You also must be ready all the time, for the Son of Man will come when least expected."

41 Peter asked, "Lord, is that illustration just for us or for everyone?"

⁴²And the Lord replied, "A faithful, sensible servant is one to whom the master can give the responsibility of managing his other household servants and feeding them. ⁴³If the master returns and finds that the servant has done a good job, there will be a reward. ⁴⁴I tell you the truth, the master will put that servant in charge of all he owns. ⁴⁵But what if the servant thinks, 'My master won't be back for a while,' and he begins beating the other servants, partying, and getting drunk? ⁴⁶The master will return unannounced and unexpected, and he will cut the servant in pieces and banish him with the unfaithful.

⁴⁷"And a servant who knows what the master wants, but isn't prepared and doesn't carry out those instructions, will be severely punished. ⁴⁸But someone who does not know, and then does something wrong, will be punished only lightly. When someone has been given much, much will be required in return; and when someone has been entrusted with much, even more will be required."

Think about the following questions and how they might apply to your life.
- In the context of this parable, how would you go about "being ready" in your life?
- What is God calling us to be ready for?
- Are you ready? Why or why not?

Hanging out with God
- Spend the next three minutes talking to God about the state of your heart. Wherever you are, God wants to hear from you. You have nothing to fear and everything to gain.

THOUGHTS

This space is here for you to jot down some thoughts, write out a prayer, draw a picture, or do whatever you want to help you remember your 10-minute moment.

Jesus is often described as a bridegroom in the Bible. It's a beautiful image, one that shows his love for us, the chosen bride. The central point here is that some of these bridesmaids weren't ready. All 10 fell asleep. All 10 brought lamps. But only five of them were prepared for the possibility that he might be late. Only five had brought extra oil. And the penalty is harsh and severe for those unprepared. Don't be caught unprepared.

2 MINUTES

Read the passage below. Circle or underline any words/phrases/ verses that you feel are important to remember.

Matthew 25:1-13

[1]*"Then the Kingdom of Heaven will be like ten bridesmaids who took their lamps and went to meet the bridegroom.* [2]*Five of them were foolish, and five were wise.* [3]*The five who were foolish didn't take enough olive oil for their lamps,* [4]*but the other five were wise enough to take along extra oil.* [5]*When the bridegroom was delayed, they all became drowsy and fell asleep.*

[6]*"At midnight they were roused by the shout, 'Look, the bridegroom is coming! Come out and meet him!'*

[7]*"All the bridesmaids got up and prepared their lamps.* [8]*Then the five foolish ones asked the others, 'Please give us some of your oil because our lamps are going out.'*

[9]*"But the others replied, 'We don't have enough for all of us. Go to a shop and buy some for yourselves.'*

10"But while they were gone to buy oil, the bridegroom came. Then those who were ready went in with him to the marriage feast, and the door was locked. *11*Later, when the other five bridesmaids returned, they stood outside, calling, 'Lord! Lord! Open the door for us!'

12"But he called back, 'Believe me, I don't know you!'

13"So you, too, must keep watch! For you do not know the day or hour of my return."

5 MINUTES

Think about the following questions and how they might apply to your life.
- What does Jesus referring to himself as a bridegroom tell us about him?
- What does it tell us about us and what our relationship is with Jesus?
- Why do you think the wise bridesmaids didn't share their oil?
- What do you think the "oil" might be in our lives today? How can we keep an extra supply?

3 MINUTES

Hanging out with God
- People may try to guess when and how Jesus will come again, but he flat-out tells us that not even the *angels* know that. So we can spend time trying to figure out something that's impossible to figure out, or we can rest in the knowledge that God has it all covered, and be prepared with the "oil" of faith, obedience, righteous living, prayer, love, and so forth.
- Thank God for his promise of Christ's return, and commit to being ready when he does.

EXPERIENCE

Ahead of time, plan to show up for something—school, work, or practice—at least five minutes early today. In that extra five minutes, stop and ask yourself: What was hard and what was easy about planning ahead? What are the benefits, and what are the costs?

THOUGHTS

This space is here for you to jot down some thoughts, write out a prayer, draw a picture, or do whatever you want to help you remember your 10-minute moment.

Day 31

THE TALENTS

Sometimes there are incredibly cool "coincidences" that happen. In Jesus' time, a talent was a coin. In our time, one of the meanings of talent is something a person is good at. This parable from Jesus is about people wasting their talents—and both meanings of the word apply here! OK, maybe nobody but a word-nerd like me thinks that's cool. But Jesus is really harsh on people who waste what they've been blessed with. "The outer darkness" is one of the most terrifying descriptions I've ever heard. I want to use my talents well, don't you?

2 MINUTES

Read the passage below. Circle or underline any words/phrases/verses that you feel are important to remember.

Matthew 25:14-30

14 "Again, the Kingdom of Heaven can be illustrated by the story of a man going on a long trip. He called together his servants and entrusted his money to them while he was gone. 15He gave five bags of silver to one, two bags of silver to another, and one bag of silver to the last—dividing it in proportion to their abilities. He then left on his trip.

16 "The servant who received the five bags of silver began to invest the money and earned five more. 17The servant with two bags of silver also went to work and earned two more. 18But the servant who received the one bag of silver dug a hole in the ground and hid the master's money.

19 "After a long time their master returned from his trip and called them to give an account of how they had used his money. 20The servant to whom he had entrusted the five bags of silver came forward with five more and said, 'Master, you gave me five bags of silver to invest, and I have earned five more.'

²¹ "The master was full of praise. 'Well done, my good and faithful servant. You have been faithful in handling this small amount, so now I will give you many more responsibilities. Let's celebrate together!'

²² "The servant who had received the two bags of silver came forward and said, 'Master, you gave me two bags of silver to invest, and I have earned two more.'

²³ "The master said, 'Well done, my good and faithful servant. You have been faithful in handling this small amount, so now I will give you many more responsibilities. Let's celebrate together!'

²⁴ "Then the servant with the one bag of silver came and said, 'Master, I knew you were a harsh man, harvesting crops you didn't plant and gathering crops you didn't cultivate. ²⁵ I was afraid I would lose your money, so I hid it in the earth. Look, here is your money back.'

²⁶ "But the master replied, 'You wicked and lazy servant! If you knew I harvested crops I didn't plant and gathered crops I didn't cultivate, ²⁷ why didn't you deposit my money in the bank? At least I could have gotten some interest on it.'

²⁸ "Then he ordered, 'Take the money from this servant, and give it to the one with the ten bags of silver. ²⁹ To those who use well what they are given, even more will be given, and they will have an abundance. But from those who do nothing, even what little they have will be taken away. ³⁰ Now throw this useless servant into outer darkness, where there will be weeping and gnashing of teeth.'"

5 MINUTES

Think about the following questions and how they might apply to your life.

- This parable is about taking risks on behalf of God—what's the difference between a good risk and a bad risk?

- What are some of your talents?
- How have you "risked" with your talents?
- What do you think God expects us to do with our talents?
- Why would God get mad at someone who gave him back just what he was given? Isn't that being responsible?

3 MINUTES

Hanging out with God
- Spend the next three minutes thanking God for the talents he's given you and asking him how he wants you to be using those talents to further his kingdom.

THOUGHTS

This space is here for you to jot down some thoughts, write out a prayer, draw a picture, or do whatever you want to help you remember your 10-minute moment.